VOLUME I
100 MANDALAS

A Mindful and Peaceful Adult Coloring Book Perfect for Stress Relief and Relaxation

Tension is who you think you should be.
Relaxation is who you are.

CHINESE PROVERB

Printed in the United States of America
First Printing, 2021
ISBN 9798723474796

Illustrations by Ioan Decean
Book design by Nicole O'Donnell
Typography: Eclipse and Secret Water

Fathead & Edmund, LLC
5260 Goldmar Drive, Irondale, AL 35210

www.fatheadandedmund.com
www.pixaroma.com

NOTHING IS LACKING

WHEN YOU REALIZE NOTHING IS LACKING,
THE WHOLE WORLD BELONGS TO YOU.

Lao Tzu

SEEK WITHIN

WHAT THE SUPERIOR MAN SEEKS IS IN HIMSELF;
WHAT THE SMALL MAN SEEKS IS IN OTHERS.

Confucius

SEEK NOTHING

To seek is to suffer.
To seek nothing is bliss.
BodHidHarma

SEEK TO UNDERSTAND

THE WISE DON'T JUDGE.
THEY SEEK TO UNDERSTAND.

Wei Wu Wei

ALL THINGS

WHEN THOUGHTS ARISE, THEN DO ALL THINGS ARISE.
WHEN THOUGHTS VANISH, THEN DO ALL THINGS VANISH.

HUANGBO XIYUN

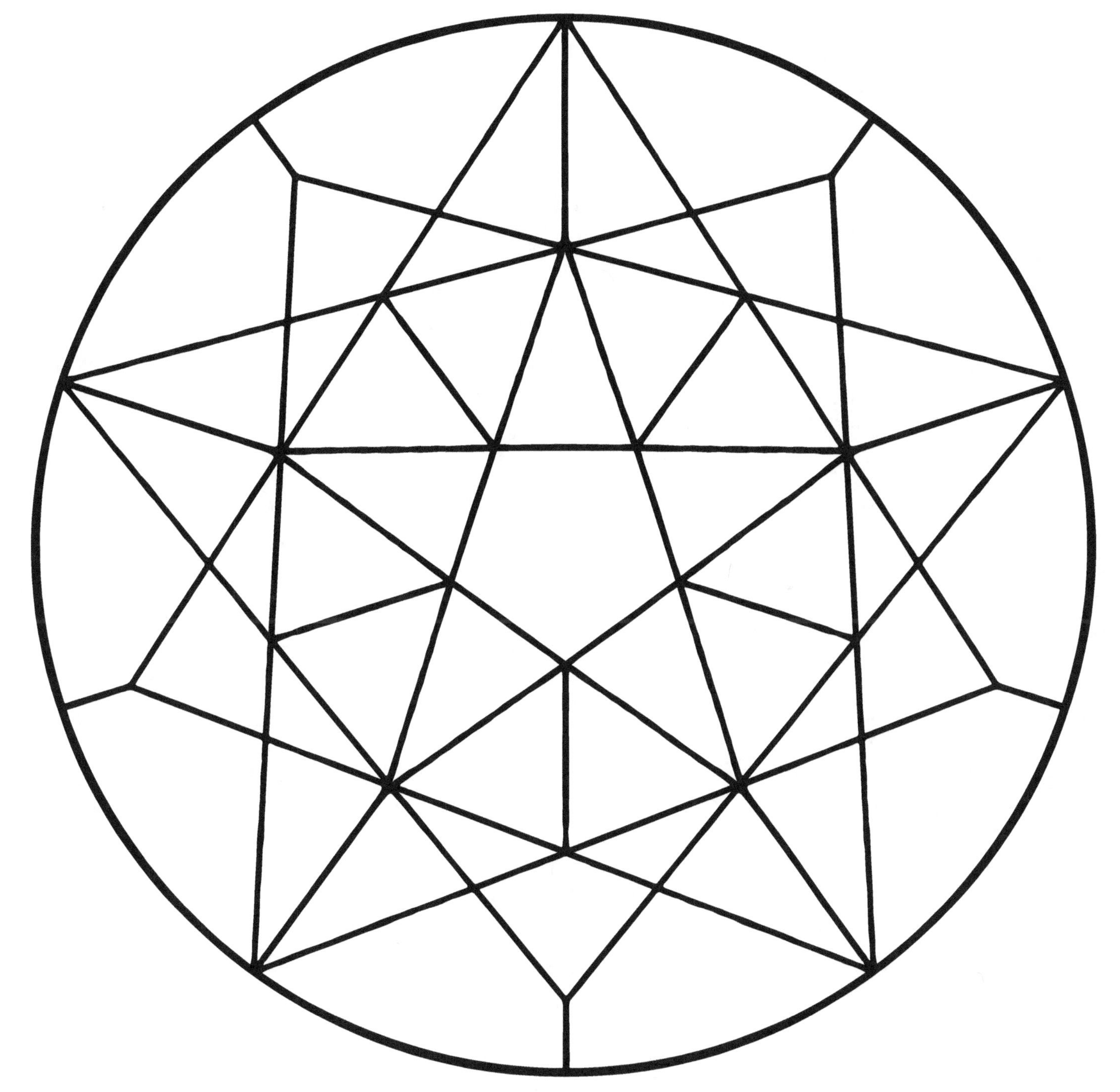

CALM AND STEADY

THE NOBLE-MINDED ARE CALM AND STEADY.
LITTLE PEOPLE ARE FOREVER FUSSING AND FRETTING.

Confucius

KNOWING

NOTHING EVER GOES AWAY UNTIL IT HAS
TAUGHT US WHAT WE NEED TO KNOW.

PEMA CHODRON

TRUTH

ONLY THE HAND THAT ERASES
CAN WRITE THE TRUTH.

MEISTER ECKHART

DISCOVERY

WHEN WE DISCOVER THAT THE TRUTH IS ALREADY IN US,
WE ARE ALL AT ONCE OUR ORIGINAL SELVES.

DOGEN

BE THERE

WHEREVER YOU ARE, BE THERE TOTALLY.

ECKHART TOLLE

THE BOUNDLESS

Forget the years, forget distinctions.
Leap into the boundless and make it your home.

ZHUANG ZHAO

THE SEARCH FOR HAPPINESS IS ONE
OF THE CHIEF SOURCES OF UNHAPPINESS.

Eric Hoffer

POSSIBILITIES

THE MIND OF THE BEGINNER IS EMPTY, FREE OF THE HABITS
OF THE EXPERT, AND OPEN TO ALL THE POSSIBILITIES.

SHUNRYU SUZUKI

BE WATER

EMPTY YOUR MIND, BE FORMLESS. SHAPELESS, LIKE WATER. . .
NOW, WATER CAN FLOW OR IT CAN CRASH. BE WATER, MY FRIEND.

BRUCE LEE

LIVE IN THE PRESENT

If you are depressed, you are living in the past.
If you are anxious, you are living in the future.
If you are at peace, you are living in the present.

Lao Tzu

PATIENCE

Do you have the patience to wait until your mud settles and the water is clear?

Lao Tzu

JUST RELAX

DON'T SEEK, DON'T SEARCH, DON'T ASK,
DON'T KNOCK, DON'T DEMAND . . . RELAX.

OSHO RAJNEESH

EVERY MOMENT

TREAT EVERY MOMENT AS YOUR LAST.
IT IS NOT PREPARATION FOR SOMETHING ELSE.
SHUNRYU SUZUKI

MIRACLES

THERE ARE ONLY TWO WAYS TO LIVE YOUR LIFE. ONE IS AS IF NOTHING IS A MIRACLE. THE OTHER IS AS IF EVERYTHING IS A MIRACLE.

ALBERT EINSTEIN

TRUE WISDOM

Knowing others is intelligence;
knowing yourself is True Wisdom.

Lao Tzu

MEMORY

To be wronged is nothing
unless you continue to remember it.

Confucius

PRACTICE COMPASSION

If you want others to be happy, practice compassion.
If you want to be happy, practice compassion.

THE 14TH DALAI LAMA

THE PRESENT MOMENT
DO NOT DWELL IN THE PAST, DO NOT DREAM OF THE FUTURE,
CONCENTRATE THE MIND ON THE PRESENT MOMENT.
GAUTAMA BUDDHA

THE WAY

All know the way, but few actually walk it.

BodHidHarma

DO NOTHING

DON'T BE AFRAID TO JUST SIT AND WATCH.

ANTHONY BOURDAIN

LOVE ALL

Love all. Serve all. Help ever. Hurt never.

SATHYA SAI BABA

TRUTH

TRUTH MAKES YOU RISE TO NEW HEIGHTS,
NO MATTER WHERE YOU ARE.

KAMAL RAVIKANT

FAILURE

A MAN IS GREAT NOT BECAUSE HE HASN'T FAILED;
A MAN IS GREAT BECAUSE FAILURE HASN'T STOPPED HIM.

CONFUCIUS

KINDNESS

Our own brain, our own heart is our temple;
the philosophy is kindness.

THE 14TH DALAI LAMA

BE FEARLESS

HAVE THE FEARLESS ATTITUDE OF A HERO
AND THE LOVING HEART OF A CHILD.

SOYEN SHAKU

LET IT GO

I FOLLOW FOUR DICTATES: FACE IT, ACCEPT IT,
DEAL WITH IT, THEN LET IT GO.

SHENG YEN

OBSERVATION

THE ability To observe WitHout evaluating
is THE HigHest form of intelligence.

Jiddu KrisHnamurti

SERENITY

Pursue not the outer entanglements; dwell not in the inner void;
be serene in the oneness of things; and dualism vanishes by itself.

Jianzhi Sengcan

MATTERS OF CONCERN

MATTERS OF GREAT CONCERN SHOULD BE TREATED LIGHTLY.
MATTERS OF SMALL CONCERN SHOULD BE TREATED SERIOUSLY.

YAMAMOTO TSUNETOMO

THE LIGHT

THERE IS A CRACK IN EVERYTHING,
THAT'S HOW THE LIGHT GETS IN.
LEONARD COHEN

EMPTINESS

WE SHAPE CLAY INTO A POT, BUT IT IS THE
EMPTINESS INSIDE THAT HOLDS WHATEVER WE WANT.

Lao Tzu

REVELATION

FOR THINGS TO REVEAL THEMSELVES TO US,
WE NEED TO BE READY TO ABANDON OUR VIEWS ABOUT THEM.

THICH NHAT HANH

WANTING

IF YOU WANT SOMETHING THEN YOU LOSE EVERYTHING. IF YOU DON'T WANT ANYTHING THEN YOU ALREADY HAVE EVERYTHING.
SEUNGSAHN

REJECTION

THE FOOLISH REJECT WHAT THEY SEE, NOT WHAT THEY THINK;
THE WISE REJECT WHAT THEY THINK, NOT WHAT THEY SEE.

HUANGBO XIYUN

CONVICTION

THE SUPREME HAPPINESS OF LIFE
IS THE CONVICTION THAT WE ARE LOVED.

VICTOR HUGO

THE MOMENT

YOU CAN HAVE THE MIND
OR YOU CAN HAVE THE MOMENT.
NAVAL RAVIKANT

DEFEAT

PREFER TO BE DEFEATED IN THE PRESENCE
OF THE WISE THAN TO EXCEL AMONG FOOLS.

DOGEN

DO NOTHING

DOING NOTHING IS BETTER
THAN BEING BUSY DOING NOTHING.

Lao Tzu

CONSCIOUSNESS

THINGS THAT HAVE A CONSCIOUSNESS ARE
HIGHER THAN THOSE THAT DON'T.

Marcus Aurelius

SILENCE

THE QUIETER YOU BECOME,
THE MORE YOU CAN HEAR.

BABA RAM DASS

HERE AND NOW

THIS IS THE REAL SECRET OF LIFE; TO BE COMPLETELY ENGAGED
WITH WHAT YOU ARE DOING IN THE HERE AND NOW.

ALAN WILSON WATTS

THE IDEAL

Life in common among people who love
each other is the ideal of happiness.

George Sand

THE PRESENT MOMENT CONTAINS THE FULLNESS OF SPACE.

SAHIL LAVINGIA

THE JOURNEY

Having no destination, I am never lost.

IKKYU SOJUN

EACH MOMENT

BE HAPPY IN THE MOMENT, THAT'S ENOUGH.
EACH MOMENT IS ALL WE NEED, NOT MORE.

MOTHER TERESA

BE EVERYWHERE

WHEN THE MIND IS NOWHERE IT IS EVERYWHERE.

ZEN PROVERB

LISTEN

If you listen completely, entirely, wholly, at the actual moment of listening there is no confusion, and that moment is enough.

Jiddu Krishnamurti

THE NEXT STEP

THE ONLY THING THAT IS ULTIMATELY REAL ABOUT YOUR JOURNEY IS THE STEP THAT YOU ARE TAKING AT THIS MOMENT. THAT'S ALL THERE EVER IS.

ECKHART TOLLE

PEACE AND UNDERSTANDING

I DO NOT WANT THE PEACE THAT PASSETH UNDERSTANDING.
I WANT THE UNDERSTANDING WHICH BRINGETH PEACE.

HELEN KELLER

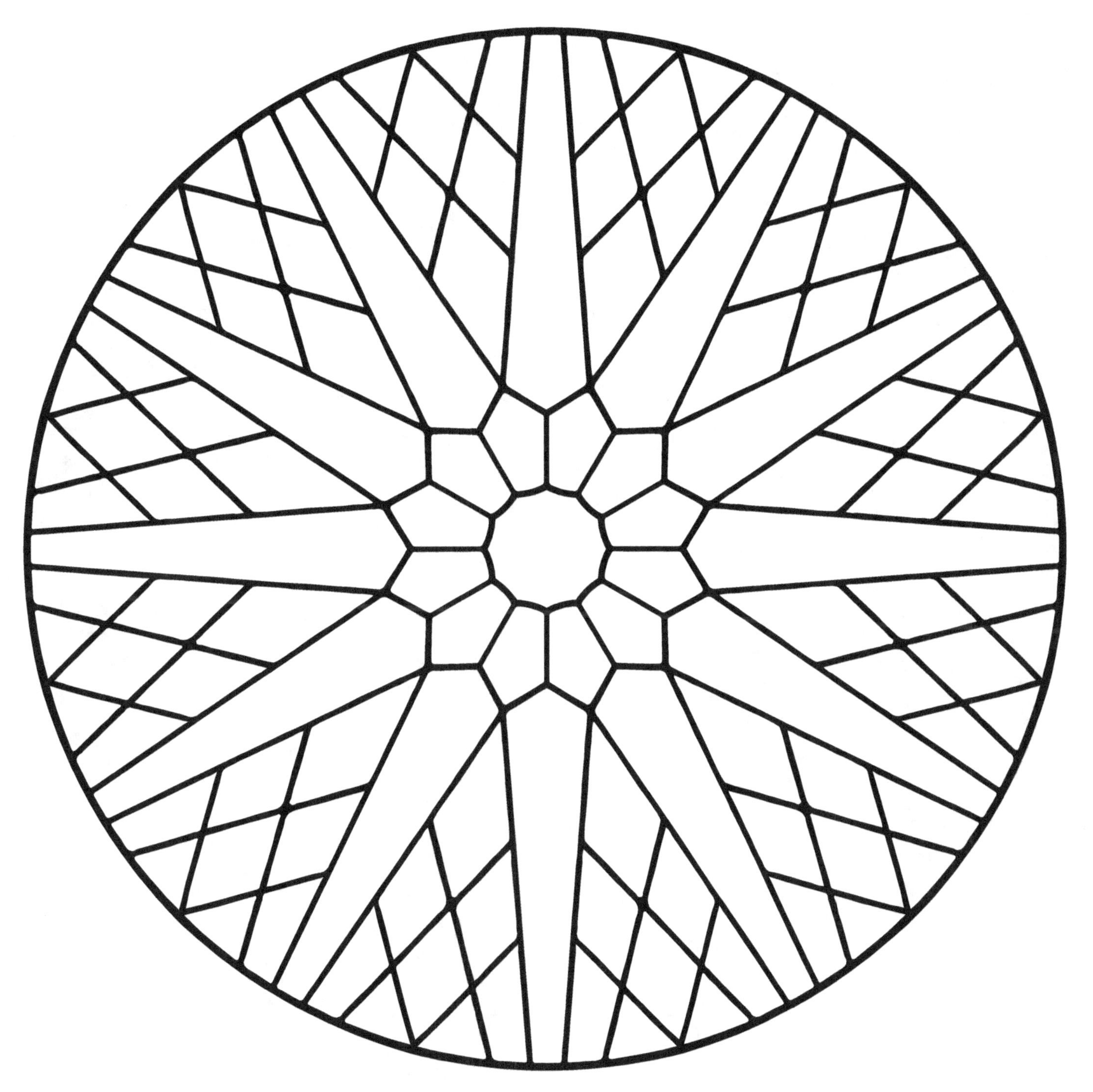

MAKE PEACE

WHEN YOU MAKE PEACE WITH YOURSELF,
YOU MAKE PEACE WITH THE WORLD.
PREAH MAHA GHOSANANDA

BE IN THE MOMENT

IF YOU AREN'T IN THE MOMENT, YOU ARE EITHER LOOKING FORWARD TO UNCERTAINTY, OR BACK TO PAIN AND REGRET.

Jim Carrey

DON'T BE AFRAID

HE WHO FEARS HE WILL SUFFER
ALREADY SUFFERS BECAUSE HE FEARS.
MICHEL DE MONTAIGNE

REST SATISFIED

True Happiness is to enjoy the present without anxious dependence upon the future, not to amuse ourselves with either hopes or fears but to rest satisfied, for He that is wants nothing.

SENECA

DON'T WORRY

WORRYING DOESN'T EMPTY TOMORROW OF ITS SORROW.
IT EMPTIES TODAY OF ITS STRENGTH.

Corrie Ten Boom

BE FREE

Today, you can decide to walk in freedom. You can choose to walk differently. You can walk as a free person, enjoying every step.

Thich Nhat Hanh

FIND PEACE

A rational person can find peace by cultivating indifference to things outside of their control.

NAVAL RAVIKANT

ACCEPTANCE

CHANGE WHAT CANNOT BE ACCEPTED
AND ACCEPT WHAT CANNOT BE CHANGED.
REINHOLD NIEBUHR

BE STILL

MOVEMENT IS GOOD FOR THE BODY.
STILLNESS IS GOOD FOR THE MIND.
SAKYONG MIPHAM RINPOCHE

MAKE TODAY YOURS

THE DAY IS ALWAYS HIS, WHO WORKS
IN IT WITH SERENITY AND GREAT AIMS.
RALPH WALDO EMERSON

DEEP SILENCE

WHEN COMPLETELY RELAXED, WE EXPERIENCE THE ESSENCE OF OUR BEING, THE DEEP SILENCE THAT KNOWS EVERYTHING AS IT IS.

HAEMIN SUNIM

WHERE YOU ARE

DECIDE THAT WHEREVER YOU ARE, IS THE BEST PLACE THERE IS.
ONCE YOU START COMPARING, THERE'S NO END TO IT.

SODO YOKOYAMA

WHAT IS PEACE?

PEACE IS THE SIMPLICITY OF HEART, THE SERENITY OF MIND,
TRANQUILITY OF SOUL, THE BOND OF LOVE.

PIO OF PIETRELCINA

HARMONY

Harmony is the feeling that arises from not wanting
to be somewhere else, doing something else.

Raj Raghunathan

STOP LEAVING AND YOU WILL ARRIVE. STOP SEARCHING AND YOU WILL SEE. STOP RUNNING AWAY AND YOU WILL BE FOUND.

Lao Tzu

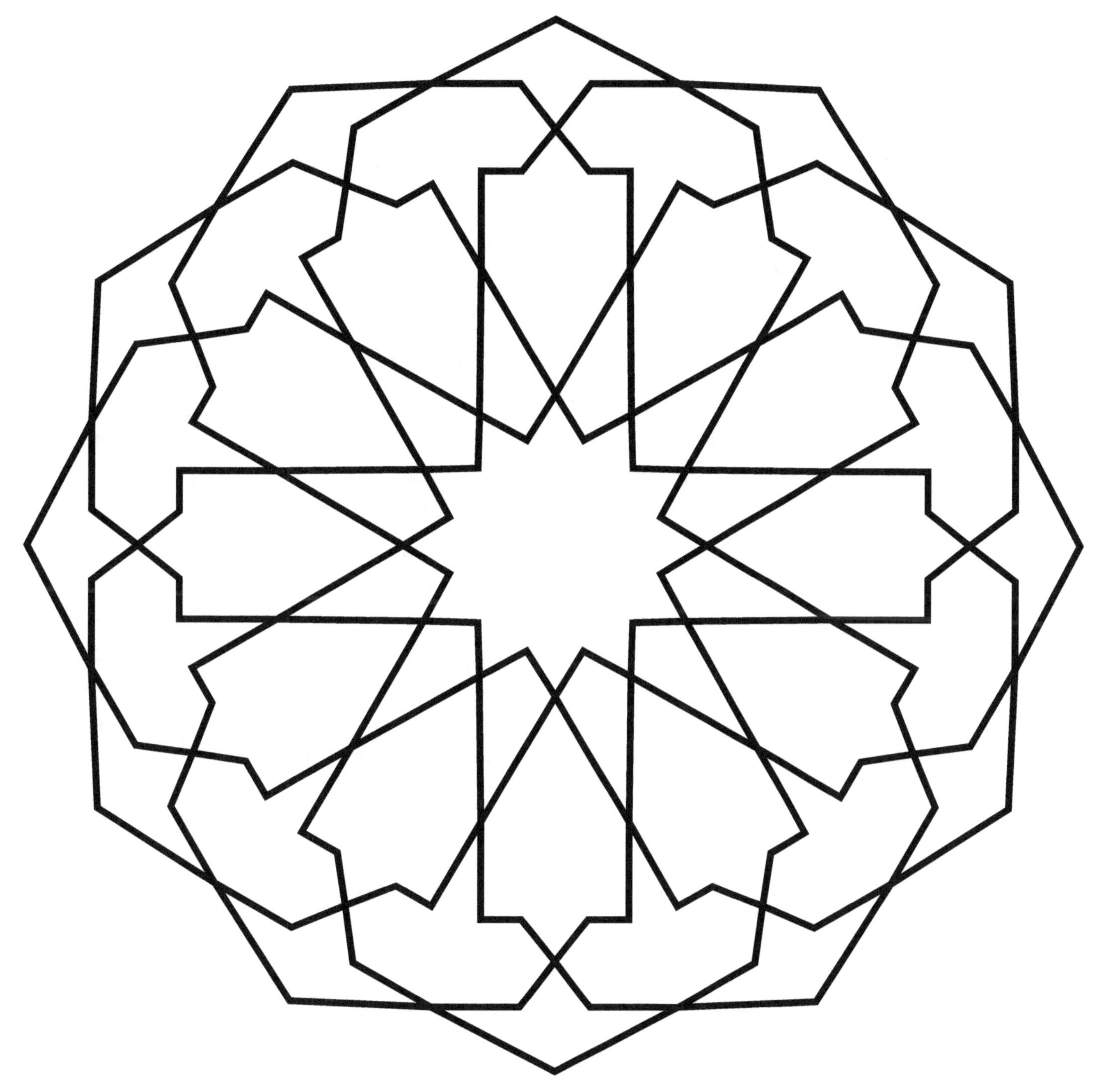

TOMORROW

TOMORROW IS A NEW DAY.
YOU SHALL BEGIN IT WELL AND SERENELY.

RALPH WALDO EMERSON

It is inner stillness that will
save and transform the world.
Eckhart Tolle

SELF CONTROL

THE SELF-CONTROLLED SOUL, WHO MOVES AMONGST SENSE OBJECTS, FREE
FROM EITHER ATTACHMENT OR REPULSION . . . WINS ETERNAL PEACE.

THE BHAGAVAD GITA

OWN YOURSELF

HE THAT OWNS HIMSELF HAS LOST NOTHING.
BUT HOW FEW MEN ARE BLESSED WITH OWNERSHIP OF SELF!

SENECA

ONLY THOSE WHO ARE FREE FROM PASSION WILL FIND DELIGHT
IN [FORESTS], FOR THEY DO NOT SEEK SENSUAL PLEASURES.

THE DHAMMAPADA

TRANQUILITY

WE CAN BE SERENE EVEN IN THE MIDST OF CALAMITIES
AND, BY OUR SERENITY, MAKE OTHERS MORE TRANQUIL.
SWAMI SATCHIDANANDA SARASWATI

TRUE FREEDOM

THE ONE WHO IS FREE OF EVERY AND ANY INTENTION,
EVEN THE INTENTION TO BE FREE, IS FREE INDEED.

Mooji

THE HIGHEST FORM OF GRACE IS SILENCE.
IT IS ALSO THE HIGHEST SPIRITUAL INSTRUCTION.
RAMANA MAHARSHI

THE MUSIC OF THE EARTH

IF WE ATTEND TO THE MUSIC OF THE EARTH, WE REACH SERENITY.
AND THEN, IN SOME UNEXPLAINED WAY, WE SHARE IT WITH OTHERS.

GLADYS TABER

THE BEGINNING AND END

PEACE DOESN'T REQUIRE TWO PEOPLE; IT REQUIRES ONLY ONE.
IT HAS TO BE YOU. THE PROBLEM BEGINS AND ENDS THERE.

BYRON KATIE

TRANQUILITY

Great tranquility of heart is his
who cares for neither praise nor blame.

Thomas A. Kempis

SIMPLICITY

THERE ARE TWO WAYS TO GET ENOUGH. ONE IS TO CONTINUE TO ACCUMULATE MORE AND MORE. THE OTHER IS TO DESIRE LESS.

G.K. CHESTERTON

WHAT IS FREEDOM?
NO DRIVES, NO COMPULSIONS, NO NEEDS, NO ATTRACTIONS;
WHEN YOUR AFFAIRS ARE UNDER CONTROL YOU ARE FREE.
ZHUANG ZHOU

THE WAY OF LOVE

THE WAY OF LOVE IS THE WAY OF NO-EXPECTATION. LOVE EXISTS ONLY
WHEN THERE IS A TOTAL ACCEPTANCE AND NO DESIRE TO CHANGE ANYTHING.

OSHO RAJNEESH

THE DUTY

THERE IS NO DUTY WE SO MUCH
UNDERRATE AS THE DUTY OF BEING HAPPY.
ROBERT LOUIS STEVENSON

ENJOY

ENJOY WHAT YOU CAN AND IGNORE THE REST. LET'S NOT WASTE ANY ENERGY FIGHTING THINGS THAT ARE OUTSIDE OUR CONTROL.
PAULO COELHO

STRENGTH

SOME OF US THINK HOLDING ON MAKES US STRONG, BUT SOMETIMES IT IS LETTING GO.

HERMAN HESSE

TRUE WISDOM

WHEN HUNGRY, EAT YOUR RICE; WHEN TIRED CLOSE YOUR EYES.
FOOLS MAY LAUGH AT ME, BUT WISE MEN WILL KNOW WHAT I MEAN.

Linji Yixuan

PAST AND FUTURE

Holding on is believing that there's only a past;
letting go is knowing that there's a future.

DAPHNE ROSE KINGMA

THE PURSUIT

THE PURSUIT, EVEN OF THE BEST THINGS,
OUGHT TO BE CALM AND TRANQUIL.

CICERO

YOUR MIND

If you can win over your mind,
you can win over the whole world.

Sri Sri Ravi Shankar

MY UNHAPPINESS WAS THE UNHAPPINESS
OF A PERSON WHO COULD NOT SAY NO.
DAZAI OZAMU

ONE SUCCESS

THERE IS ONLY ONE SUCCESS: TO BE ABLE
TO SPEND YOUR LIFE IN YOUR OWN WAY.
CHRISTOPHER MORLEY

UNDERSTANDING

NO HUMAN BEING CAN REALLY UNDERSTAND ANOTHER,
AND NO ONE CAN ARRANGE ANOTHER'S HAPPINESS.
GRAHAM GREENE

WORDS AND THOUGHTS

MY WORDS FLY UP, MY THOUGHTS REMAIN BELOW:
WORDS WITHOUT THOUGHTS NEVER TO HEAVEN GO.

WILLIAM SHAKESPEARE

WRONG AND RIGHT

Out beyond ideas of wrongdoing and rightdoing there is a field. I'll meet you there.

Rumi

LEARNING

LEARNING TO LET GO SHOULD BE LEARNED BEFORE LEARNING TO GET.
LIFE SHOULD BE TOUCHED, NOT STRANGLED. YOU'VE GOT TO RELAX,
LET IT HAPPEN AT TIMES, AND AT OTHERS MOVE FORWARD WITH IT.

RAY BRADBURY

THE SILENCE WITHIN

To preserve the silence within--amid all the noise. To remain open and quiet, a moist humus in the fertile darkness where the rain falls and the grain ripens--no matter how many tramp across the parade ground in whirling dust under an arid sky.

Dag Hammarskjold

THE PATH

WALK AS IF YOU ARE KISSING THE EARTH WITH YOUR FEET.

THICH NHAT HANH

INVENTION
WHEN THE MIND IS EXHAUSTED OF IMAGES,
IT INVENTS ITS OWN.
GARY SNYDER

ASK

ALWAYS ASK YOURSELF:
"WHAT WILL HAPPEN IF I SAY NOTHING?"
KAMAND KOJOURI